Prayers for *Dementia*

FAY SAMPSON

NOVALIS
TWENTY-THIRD PUBLICATIONS
twentythirdpublications.com

Published in Canada by Novalis
Publishing Office
10 Lower Spadina Avenue, Suite 400
Toronto, Ontario, Canada
M5V 2Z2

Head Office
4475 Frontenac Street
Montréal, Québec, Canada
H2H 2S2

www.novalis.ca

Cover design and layout: Audrey Wells
Cover image: iStockphoto

Cataloguing in Publication is available from Library and Archives Canada.
ISBN: 978-2-89688-442-1
We acknowledge the support of the Government of Canada.
Printed in Canada.

Published in the United States by
TWENTY-THIRD PUBLICATIONS
One Montauk Avenue, Suite 200
New London, CT 06320
(860) 437-3012 or (800) 321-0411
www.twentythirdpublications.com
ISBN: 978-1-62785-400-9

Originally published in the UK by
Darton, Longman and Todd
140-142 Wandsworth High Street
London SW18 4JJ
ISBN: 978-0-232-53297-5

Cover design: Jeff McCall
Cover image: ©Shutterstock.com

5 4 3 2 1 22 21 20 19 18

Table of Contents

About This Book

Better health care means that many of us are living longer. This carries with it an increased probability that more of us will develop dementia, or will know someone who has.

The prayers in this book are divided into three groups. The first group is for the use of those with dementia. The second is for caregivers. And the final prayers are for the use of family, friends and the wider community. But you can use any of them with, or on behalf of, someone else.

You may wish to insert *him* or *her* or a personal name, in place of a more general term like the one I love or the one living with dementia.

The prayers are accompanied by information about dementia and the best way to handle its symptoms. It has not been possible to cover every aspect of this large subject. You may wish to add prayers of your own which relate to your particular experience. You may also wish to add notes about other resources you have found helpful to hand on to others.

And remember that normal life doesn't come to a standstill when someone is diagnosed with dementia. Make the most of the time you have.

PART A

For the use of, or on behalf of, those with dementia

"And you know the way to the place where I am going."
Thomas said to him, "Lord,
we do not know where you are going.
How can we know the way?"
Jesus said to him, "I am the way,
and the truth, and the life."

John 14.4-6

Lord Jesus, hold my hand.

They tell me I have dementia, but that can't be true. All right, my memory is not what it used to be, but I'm as sane as anyone else. I'm not demented.

I've seen people with dementia. I'm not like that. Most of the time, I function perfectly well.

But the test results are in, and they say that's what I have.

I'm frightened, Lord. It's not something I ever imagined happening to me. I fear the loss of my identity. I dread the falling away of what I know and can do. Put your arm around me as I journey into the unknown.

If it is true, then I am going to need help. Give me people around me who understand my anxiety about the path I must tread. May the light in your smile assure me of my continued worth in your eyes, just as you loved and valued me when I was a helpless baby. Affirm me in all that I am and have been, even if others see only my decline.

"Are not five sparrows sold for two pennies?
Yet not one of them is forgotten in God's sight.
But even the hairs of your head are all counted.
Do not be afraid; you are of more value
than many sparrows."

Luke 12.6-7

Shepherd of my path,

so I have dementia. Give me grace to accept this as part of the pattern of my life and that of many others. May I enjoy the present moment and all the life I have yet to live.

Grant me the humility to accept the assistance I will need. I give you gratitude for all those I am finding who so readily offer that help.

Lord, you walked an unwelcome path you feared into a dark unknown. It took a greater courage than mine to do that willingly. In my darkening path, take me by the hand and share your courage with me.

Can a woman forget her nursing child, or show no compassion for the child of her womb?
Even these may forget, yet I will not forget you.

Isaiah 49.15

Faithful God,

my memory is not what it used to be. I forget things. I forget people. But they do not forget me.

I give you heartfelt thanks that I have people around me who love me and care for me. They understand what is happening to me.

Always I have you beside me.

You show me that it does not really matter if I forget things. I'm allowed to.

Give me the grace to see that the present is enough for me. I still have the sunrise on a frosty garden. I still enjoy my favourite food. I have not lost the gift of laughter. I have someone to guide me where I need to go.

And I have my memories of the past, which seem to grow more vivid day by day.

Let me meet the days ahead with trust and serenity. Bless all those who walk beside me.

Hold my hand.

PART B

For the use of,
or on behalf of,
caregivers

Seeking Help

You notice that someone close to you is becoming increasingly forgetful. At first, you put it down to advancing years. Then gradually you realize that these lapses of memory can no longer be laughed off as 'senior moments.' A more serious change is happening to the one you love.

If this is dementia, then you know this change is going to be irreversible. The two of you are embarking on a journey that may be sad, bewildering, even scary. You would rather close your mind to it.

But take courage. You are not alone. A host of people are waiting to help you along this way. The sooner you and your loved one entrust yourselves to them, the better the outcome will be for both of you. There may be medication which can help. There is advice on living well with dementia. Don't miss this opportunity.

You will need to take the initiative. Encourage the one you are concerned for to report these memory problems to their doctor. Accompany them to reassure them.

You are likely to be referred to a specialist clinic. There will probably be a period of memory tests and possibly a brain scan before you get a firm diagnosis. This is precious time. Value each moment.

Guiding God,

your Son gathered tremendous reserves of courage in the wilderness to meet the road ahead. Let me have the courage to face the fact that we need professional help. Show me that true love lies not in denial or false hopes, but in caring honesty. Let me be the one to realize that the best future for the one I love lies in facing up to this moment.

Reassure me that abundant help and support is waiting. First and foremost, there is the strength of your ever-loving arms. Then take us both by the hand and lead us to the place where practical help can start.

We have your gift of time in front of us. Let us not waste a day by denying the truth.

We shall both need your bravery, your wisdom, your patience and understanding in the days to come. Bless us as we take the first uncertain steps into this new phase of our life.

The Word "Dementia"

"Cancer" used to be the word no one spoke. Now it is out there, upfront. Relatives and friends don pink ribbons, run marathons or shave their heads to raise funds for cancer care and research.

Yet there is still reluctance to say the word "dementia." It is part of the lingering stigma around mental illness. It can be difficult for someone with dementia to accept the diagnosis. It may be easier to talk about 'memory loss' when persuading a loved one to seek help. You will want to be tactful with the one who has dementia, but be honest with everyone else.

Dementia is as much a physical illness as cancer. Changes are happening to the brain, and these affect behaviour and abilities. Someone who has dementia needs understanding and help. Research into its causes and treatment also needs money, just as cancer research does. There is a new movement to bring dementia upfront. People can sign up to become a 'dementia friend,' and wear a badge to raise awareness. People with dementia are encouraged to carry a card to say so, so that they can ask for extra patience at the cash, or anywhere else where everyday tasks become confusing and they need more time.

So many people have dementia nowadays that it need no longer be seen as abnormal. Being honest about it and spreading understanding are the best ways to improve the quality of life for the one you love and for many others.

Truthful Christ,

you made your disciples face the hard facts they did not want to hear. Help me meet this unwanted diagnosis of dementia in the same way I would any other illness. Give me the wisdom and tact I will need to help the one I love come to terms with this new word in our lives. May the arms of your love, and my own, be there to support and help them as they learn to accept this reality.

Grant me the openness to be one who seeks to change popular perceptions by accepting the word "dementia" and speaking honestly about it. Through our lives, may I and the one I care for show others that this is a serious problem, but that there can still be much joyful life ahead for both of us.

With your grace, may I and all the others in this situation bring this word out of the shadows to be seen as part of the lives of very many people.

You never shrank back from telling the truth. May my honesty help others to accept and understand the reality of dementia.

Understanding Dementia

He was driving with his wife along the familiar road into town. Suddenly he exclaimed, "I don't know where I am!" He pulled over to the side of the road and never drove again.

Dementia takes a variety of forms. One of the most common, Alzheimer's, usually involves a steady decline. Its progress may be slowed by medication.

On the other hand, vascular dementia, another common type, typically proceeds in steps. The person who has it may remain on one level for some time, and then suffer an abrupt loss of ability without warning, like the car driver who suddenly found himself in an unfamiliar world. The condition may then plateau before the next sudden decline.

There are other forms, like Lewy body dementia, which may lead to hallucinations. A farmer watched a procession of tractors trundle along the hospital ward. Terry Pratchett had a rare form of dementia which allowed him to go on writing best-selling novels with a little help from his friends.

Someone with serious memory problems may be given a brain scan. This can help determine what sort of dementia it is.

Once you have a diagnosis, abundant support is on hand to help you understand what is happening. You will be given literature to tell you more. You will probably be invited to attend classes where you will learn more about dementia and the best way to live with it. You will share experiences with others living with this condition and their caregivers. Some people find it hard to accept the diagnosis, and they react with fear. There is support to help them come to terms with it.

In the first shock of diagnosis, it is easy to back away and say, "I don't want to think about it." But love for the person you care for involves understanding as much about their condition as you can, so that you know how best you may help them.

God of Compassion,

you gave your time, your energy, to those in need. Grant me wisdom to understand more about what is happening to the one I love.

I give you thanks for the abundance of resources available to help those with dementia and their caregivers. I see your love in the professionals, the volunteers, the fundraisers, the researchers. May I take with both hands the help that is offered to us.

Let me not be so bound up with my own problems that I neglect to give time, enthusiasm and money to increase the help available to us and to others. Show me how best I may support the efforts already being made. Make me an advocate for the greater understanding of dementia in the community. Help me to turn what is happening to us into a positive for us and for others.

Memory

One of the earliest signs that the changes taking place may be dementia, and not just the increasing forgetfulness common in old age, is repeatedly asking the same question. Short-term memory is what goes first. Even when you know that it is due to physical deterioration of the brain, it can be exasperating. It can be hard to keep the impatience out of your voice as you answer the same question for the seventh time in as many minutes.

There is nothing you or the one you love can do about this. You simply have to accept it as the new normal. You need to lower your expectations. It's not so irritating if you know this is going to happen. You simply learn to answer the question patiently, as often as it takes.

But there are things you can do to help. Don't burden the other person with more information than they need. Try to take life one step at a time. There is no need to discuss arrangements for what you are going to do tomorrow. It will only lead to a series of questions like: "Where are we going?" "What time is the train?" "Who are we going to see?" each repeated multiple times. In your dealings with the other person, let tomorrow take care of itself.

Repeated questions may also be a sign of stress. Do everything you can to relieve them of anxiety about the thing that is worrying them.

Loving God,

you have been more patient with me and with humanity than we could ever expect or deserve. Grant me the same loving patience.

Let me view failing memory with the same compassion as I would a greater difficulty in walking. Help me to be supportive, not demanding. School me to control my voice, so that I answer the seventh identical question as sympathetically as I did the first.

May I never be guilty of sounding as though this failure of memory is the fault of the one I love.

And when I fail, continue to be patient with me.

Preparing for the Future

Most of us have a list of things we know we should do, but haven't got around to yet. A diagnosis of dementia brings a new urgency to this. People with dementia may function quite well at the moment, but the time will come when they no longer have the capacity to make legally binding decisions. It's important for them to get their affairs in order while they can. And it's a good idea for their caregiver to do the same for themselves.

If you haven't already made a will, now is the time to do this, or to check if an existing will needs updating.

But dementia does not mean death is imminent. The person with dementia may live for decades. Yet their abilities will decline. Someone else will need to have the power to make decisions about their financial affairs and health management in the future.

Both the cared-for and the caregiver need to set up Enduring Powers of Attorney for financial and property affairs, and for health and welfare. You don't need a lawyer for this. Forms are available online.

Support services are available for people with dementia, but also for those who care for them. Carry a card in your wallet saying that you are a caregiver. If you have an accident, people will know that there is someone at home who is relying on you.

You will be encouraged to draw up an emergency plan. This will list family or friends who live nearby and who can step in to cover for you until longer-term plans can be made. Some groups provide containers in which you keep a care plan for the one you look after. The fridge is the recommended place to keep it.

Now may be the time to think about where you live. Do you have a network of friends you can rely on? Would you rather be near other family members? Do you have access to public transit? It's a big decision to move while the person with dementia is not too seriously affected. But if you are going to do it, it's best to get on with it. The longer you leave it, the harder it will be for the person you care for to come to terms with unfamiliar surroundings.

When all the practical provisions have been made, you can relax and get on with enjoying your lives.

Journeying God,

our lives have altered. There are so many things to think about, so much to come to terms with. Guide me to make the practical decisions that we must.

You know our weakness and our reluctance. We would like to pretend we can go on living as we do now. It is hard to look to the future and acknowledge how much things must change. Be the Shepherd who leads us into the unknown. Let us do all we can to ease that transition into a new way of life.

When we have done everything that we can think of, grant us the serenity to trust the rest to your hands.

Rapid-onset Dementia

Typically, dementia develops over a period of years. Caregivers and family have time to adjust and plan for the future.

But it is not the same for everyone. The onset can be sudden and the deterioration rapid. This is particularly hard for their partner. Before they know where they are, the one they love is in a nursing home, barely able to speak intelligibly and having difficulty walking. This no longer seems like the person they have shared their life with. There has been no time for that lingering, affectionate farewell that long-term caregivers are able to make. It is like a sudden bereavement.

There is no simple answer, no easy consolation. The partner will need time to grieve this unexpected and very real loss. Friends can accompany them on this journey, but they cannot fully share the pain.

All the grieving partner can do is show the warmth of their love when they visit. Hold a hand. Talk, whether there is any response or not. Read a favourite poem, or the sports page of a newspaper. Play music. We need to believe that our loving presence carries its own message. If possible, allow yourself the support of one or two close friends. Let them filter news of your partner to the rest of your circle. Give yourself permission to talk to them about how you feel.

Above all, let taking it to God in prayer not be a clichéd response but a reality.

Dear God,

Why me? Why do I see other people accompanying their loved ones on a long, gentle journey, while I have the one I love torn from me so suddenly?

I don't understand what has happened to us. I wasn't prepared for this.

Am I being selfish? Did I think we two should be spared such pain in a world like this? I don't know what to think, only that I am hurting.

Give me the courage to lift my eyes and see those who have been truly bereaved. Let me understand more truly how much that hurt. Join my prayers, my tears, to theirs.

Suffering Christ, you saw everything dear to you ripped away in Gethsemane. You, above all, understand what I am feeling.

Hold my hand and give me strength. May I go on holding the hand of the one dear to me and expressing my love no matter what.

May I lay my head on your shoulder and weep the tears I do not want anyone else to see.

Community

If you are caring for someone with dementia, the support of friends is invaluable. As the condition grows more severe, the person you are caring for will need to be accompanied wherever they go. They will become increasingly passive, and lose the incentive to seek out company for themselves.

You will be particularly fortunate if you belong to a church. There you will have a caring community. There will be people, clergy and lay, who see befriending those in need as part of their vocation. They will visit on a regular basis. The church community will pray for you.

It is likely that someone with dementia will be able to attend church for years to come and meet with sympathetic friends. Some may offer to come over and sit with that person, giving the caregiver a chance to get out alone or to meet with friends. They may offer to take the friend with dementia out without their caregiver.

A network of friends can be enormously helpful. Yet former friends may withdraw, because they feel they won't know what to say. Those who once shared a common interest, like bridge or singing in a choir, may fade away as the one with dementia no longer keeps up that interest. The caregiver may need to take the initiative in inviting them to visit and revive these memories.

You may find it helpful to join a new group which includes others in the same position. They may meet for coffee or tea and a chat. It may be a walking group with a not-too-demanding program. Some groups do a great job of getting people together to enjoy making music, particularly songs which bring back memories. Music can stimulate people who are losing interest in the world around them.

There are groups just for caregivers. If you are feeling lonely and burdened, it can help to meet up with others in a similar situation. You can compare notes, realize others are having a harder time than you, and exchange helpful information. Or, simply free yourself to laugh at some of the things that happen.

Don't be too proud to admit that you need support.

Loving Christ,

you shared your burdens with your friends. Help me to cherish our friends. May I not be afraid to show them how they can help.

You know how often I feel tired and overburdened. It can seem an effort to try a new group. Give me the wisdom to see that the one I am caring for needs whatever enrichment our community can provide to prolong the quality of life. Strengthen me with the courage, the energy, to seek out such friends, old and new. Grant me the humility to realize that I need not do it all by myself.

But you suffered the pain of friends who let you down. I struggle to forgive those friends who have dropped away because the one whose society they enjoyed now has dementia. Heal the pain to me and to the one I love. Grant me your compassion.

And thank you, caring Christ, that there is so much support for people like us. Give me the grace to accept it with open hands.

Aggression

Some of the changes which dementia may bring are harder to cope with than others, both for the one with dementia and for their caregivers. Not everyone regresses sweetly into childhood. There can be personality changes. The person with dementia may become aggressive. A cousin's husband once threw her down the stairs.

This can be upsetting and even frightening.

Remember that the one behaving aggressively may themselves be frightened. Their world is becoming increasingly bewildering. They may have a need they are unable to communicate and which is not being met. Remain calm. Don't take it personally. Check for practical causes. Are they physically uncomfortable in some way? Are their glasses or hearing aids working properly? Has someone behaved inappropriately to them?

Don't rebuke them. They urgently need your love and reassurance. This can be especially hard if they have threatened you physically.

Above all, don't try to cope with this on your own. Professionals are used to handling this behaviour. There are volunteers on the end of a phone. Seek the emotional support of family and friends. Both of you need help and care.

Lord, I'm in difficulty.

For years, I've coped with memory loss in the one I love. I've done my best to keep them contented and assured of my love. Now they shout at me and threaten me. I no longer recognize the relationship between us.

I know I should be praying for them. But I need help myself. I feel bewildered, confused and frightened. Put your arms around me and reassure me. Hold me back from retaliating with angry words. Give me calm and understanding.

It's a shock to be treated like this. Why would they behave like this to one who has loved them? But you know more than I can ever see, and can still less experience. In your mercy, you love each of us unconditionally. You went to the Cross for both of us.

Heal the hurts this aggression causes us. Give me, and others, wisdom to know what is upsetting the one I love.

If I can't take away the cause of this aggression, then give me the patience, the courage, the caring heart to continue giving the love I did before.

I thank you in your mercy that now, when I need it most, there are those I can call upon to help. Give me the humility to accept that I cannot cope with this on my own.

I certainly cannot cope with this without you.

Moving On

Most families want, or feel they ought to, care for the one they love as long as they can. But as the years go by, the dementia is likely to be accompanied by other frailties of old age. Having dementia makes it harder to cope. It may cause difficult behaviour problems. If the caregiver is the same age, then they, too, will feel the effects of growing older.

It is hard for a family to make the decision that the time has come for that loved person to move into long-term care. It can feel like abdicating from a responsibility. We do not want to take the one we love away from all that is familiar to them. We fear that, however good and kind the staff are, they cannot love that person as we do. It feels selfish to acknowledge how much easier this will make our own lives.

The one living with dementia may have been in a nursing home for a short time to give their caregiver a break. It's a good way to test possible future options. But it's a different matter to make that permanent decision. Professional support workers may be better at judging that moment than family. It can be both hard and a relief to accede to their greater wisdom and experience. We will be saying goodbye to a large part of our lives. We fear we may not have made the right decision. We know in our heads that this has become necessary, but the relief is still shadowed by guilt.

Dear Christ,

you know what it is like to reach a crossroads in your life where you must make an irrevocable decision. You suffered the far greater agony of that in Gethsemane.

Look with compassion on me now. My fear is that the one I love will suffer if I make the wrong choice. I feel I should go on shouldering the burden. It seems wrong to accept the freedom and release of letting go. Help me to see with clarity and wisdom what is truly in the best interests of the one I have cared for.

Merciful Lord, grant me the humility to accept when I can no longer cope, when others can do it better. Take away the guilt and replace it with a grateful heart.

Visiting

There, it's done. The person I have cared for so long is now being looked after by others. But the guilt doesn't go away. I wonder how they are adjusting. Are they happy, bored, well looked after? How much do they miss me?

The guilt doesn't end when you have decided to put a spouse or a parent into care. You try to assuage that guilt by visiting as often as you can. If it's a spouse or a long-term partner, you may feel you should visit every day. If you live further away, you will wonder how often you can and should make the journey.

The most common symptom of dementia is memory loss. Though you may be haunted by remembrance of the one who is no longer there, they themselves may not have such a clear memory of you. Since they do not know what day it is, they will have no idea when you last visited. Time has narrowed down to the present, or more likely the remembered past.

If your visits give them pleasure, then of course you will want to go as often as you can. You may be able to take them out. You can reminisce with them about things you both enjoyed. You can show them they are still loved. You can laugh with them.

But as time goes by, the link between you is likely to weaken. They may struggle to remember who you are. The things that once gave them pleasure may leave them unresponsive. You may sit there, holding their hand, even talking to them, without being sure that they know you are there.

It may be the staff at the long-term care home who tell you gently that you really don't need to come every day. It won't make a difference if you miss occasionally, if you start to leave longer spaces between your visits, or if you stay for a shorter time.

You want to surround them with your love for as long as possible. Yet, as the one you love drifts away from you, you may need to give yourself permission to let them go.

God, to Whom the Shadows and the Light Are Both Alike,

take the one I love into your arms as they enter this dark valley. Accompany them where I no longer can.

I feel a sense of bereavement. It seems as though the one I care for is no longer there. I cannot know what it feels like, or how much they feel at all.

Grant me the healing of that loss. Give them peace. Give me peace. I let them go into your hands.

PART C

For the use of family, friends and the wider community

Family

In today's world, it is common for members of the same family to live a long distance apart. If a parent develops dementia, this leads to anxiety for the children. There is greater urgency if that parent lives alone. Someone needs to be on hand to see they look after themselves, that they live safely and take their medication. A neighbour or close friend may be prepared to keep an eye on them. A health worker may visit daily.

But the time will come when this is no longer enough. Then it's decision time. Should you invite your parent to live with you? This will be influenced by whether you have a spare room, and whether you, and possibly your partner, are able to combine looking after your parent with your job commitments. If not, is one of you prepared, and financially able, to leave their job? Are there children involved?

What about the rest of the family? You will all need to ask yourselves the same questions. There can be tension if someone feels others are not doing their share.

If your parent and you agree that a long-term care home is the best option, should it be near you, or where they now live and where they may have a circle of supportive friends?

These are big decisions, but you are not alone. Commit it to prayer. Seek the practical advice of those who are familiar with this situation.

Parenting God,

your Son was born in a stable, totally dependent on human parents. I now find my own parent in that state of dependence. I want to offer them the best future I can. This may mean sacrifices of my time, my freedom, my patience, my care. It may call for sacrifices from other people. Guide me with tact and wisdom as we discuss this together.

May my home be a place of loving welcome as long as my parent needs it.

Grant me the wise support of professionals who can see more clearly than I do what would be best.

If a care home is going to be the best outcome, then help me choose that home with a view to their greatest happiness. May I involve my parent in that choice as much as I can.

Give all of us the wisdom to handle the financial decisions this will involve.

Loving Father, show me what is best, then give me the grace to embrace the decision we have made with warmth and loving humour.

I commit my increased responsibility to you. Give me grace to undertake this role reversal, to care for the one who cared for me. May the Spirit direct me and the rest of the family as we plan for my parent's future. May we listen for your voice and trust its wisdom.

The Other Parent

A set of decisions needs to be made for a parent with dementia living alone. But if both parents are alive and still together, the situation is different. You will need to stand back a little and let the other parent make most of the choices. But that won't stop you feeling concerned. And the caregiving parent will need your support.

In most cases, your other parent will be able, and will probably want, to care for the one with dementia.

But both are getting older. It is likely that one or both of them has other health problems. The parent without dementia may already be feeling the need to ease their workload. Yet now they have to take on tasks which previously fell to their spouse. Life will be harder and lonelier.

If you live some distance away, it may be difficult to know what you can do to help. Certainly keep in touch more often than you used to. It will be a help for the caring parent to unload all the exasperations and inconveniences of living with someone with dementia, however much they love them. The parent with dementia may develop irritating habits, like losing keys or coats. They may neglect to take their medication. They may put things away where they can't be found. The caregiver may turn around in a crowded public space and find that their partner is missing. These may not be major disasters, but they can take their toll. It helps to have someone to share this with, even if there is nothing you can do to change things.

If you live near enough, you can make more frequent visits to help out with those extra tasks. If you are further away, you may need to come and stay more often, even though that can be hard in a busy life.

Give both of them pleasure with your presence when you can. Only if you are in constant touch can you be sensitive to whether the time has come for the parent with dementia to move into residential care. This can be a hard choice for the caring parent. You will need tact and wisdom to help shoulder this burden. And of course, you will pray for them both daily.

God of Boundless Strength,

look with compassion on my parents, who are struggling with this situation. Give me the grace to see what I can do to help, and to offer that help willingly.

May my caregiver parent know the certainty of your presence and strength. Give them wisdom to make the choices that will be best for both of them. May your loving Spirit fill the change in their relationship. Comfort that sense of bereavement.

I trust you to hold the hand of my parent with dementia. I can imagine only a little of how it feels to enter that mental fog. Assure them how much I love and value them. Help me to cherish the past we shared and bring it to mind for their enjoyment. Let me make the happiness of both of them my priority.

Let me be a rock when they need it. Let me awaken laughter when things are getting them down. May they know I will always be there for them, as you are always here for me.

Friends

In today's aging population, more of us find that we know someone with dementia.

What can we do? If we have not had close experience of dementia, we may feel hesitant about communicating with someone in that situation. What do we say? What help would be welcome?

Dementia is usually a slow decline. For some time to come, the person who has it will still be able to converse normally to a large degree. But don't expect them to make the sort of contributions they used to. You will need to take the initiative.

They will have trouble remembering what they did five minutes ago. But if you touch on memories from the past, your friend is more likely to respond. They may have forgotten what happened this morning, but have a vivid recall of their younger days. There may be experiences the two of you shared which you can use.

If you haven't seen that person for a while, it may be a good idea to show them pictures of friends and family. Older photos may work particularly well. But offer all this as a gift, not something to be traded in an effort to stimulate a response. If you get a response, accept it gladly. Yet remember that your only aim is to make this encounter enjoyable for both of you.

You will feel sympathy for their caregiver, yet wonder what you can do to help. As it becomes increasingly difficult for the cared-for one to be left alone, you could offer to come and sit with them, or to take them out. Looking after someone with dementia can be tiring and isolating. The caregiver needs to have time on their own or the chance to meet with friends. You can make that possible.

Do all you can to make both of them feel they are still valued members of your community. Don't back away when they need you.

Hold them in your prayers.

Friend of the Friendless,

when I look around, I see a number of friends and acquaintances with dementia. It is tempting to look away and tell myself it is somebody else's problem.

Shepherding Christ, you went out of your way to find the lonely and the lost. Grant me compassion and insight to feel what it is like for someone who is losing their memory, increasingly adrift in a once familiar world. Let me be the one to hold out a hand that can anchor them to the life and friendships they knew.

Grant me the wisdom to see how I can help their caregiver, and the will and energy to act on that knowledge. Let me not make excuses. Save me from being the one who passes by on the other side of the road.

Lord, you were always ready to speak out for those in need. Guide me to find out more about dementia. Give me the commitment to be a Dementia Friend, and to advocate greater understanding in the community.

May I have your courage not to back away from the unfamiliar, but to reach out the hand of love.

Questions

If you live with someone with dementia, then you learn what works with them and what to avoid. But what if you can visit only occasionally, or meet an old friend once a week?

The thing is not to make your conversation too demanding. A polite generality, like "How are you?" may be OK. You're not really expecting a detailed answer. But avoid direct questions about what the other person has done or is going to do. "What are you doing for Christmas?" may be met with a blank stare or a look of panicked confusion. Better to chat about what you are doing.

Asking questions of someone with dementia can lead to anxiety. They feel they should know the answers to these questions, but the memory eludes them. This lowers their self-esteem.

We need to change our usual approach. Instead of asking questions, talk about subjects that once meant something to that person. Recall shared experiences, and news about family members or friends. This may trigger memories from the past, but don't demand them.

It is hard for someone with dementia to hang on to the information they already have. This makes them unlikely to ask questions to find out more about you. You will need to keep the conversation going.

My Lord and My Friend,

guide me with tact and wisdom to enrich my encounters with my friend with dementia. May I not be scared off by the fear that I won't know what to say. Fill me with your certainty that this is still the person I knew and valued. They may have forgotten our times together, or even forgotten me, but, if you will, use me to rekindle the warmth of our past.

I will need your imagination, your patience. Show me how to unlock the memories of the experiences and the people we shared. Give me the grace not to feel rejected if I get little response. Let me still be an enjoyable storyteller and companion.

As you have befriended me through thick and thin, may I make my friend feel valued by my willingness to share my time and enthusiasm with them. Give me the generosity to include them in our community in whatever way I can.

Be my faithful friend as I seek to befriend the other.

The Church

Most of us know someone with dementia, either up close or at a distance. It is likely that there will be several in your church. Naturally, we feel sympathy for them and for their caregiver, but we may not know what we can do beyond praying for them.

The important thing is to make them feel that they are fully valued as members of your community. Go out of your way to welcome them, before or after the liturgy.

Include them in group conversations, without putting too much pressure on them to contribute.

Don't sideline them. Activities in the church may be just what they need to give them a full and happy life for as long as possible. If they seem to be dropping out, give them a special invitation to an activity. Perhaps offer to pick them up.

Don't underestimate their abilities. If they used to be a reader at Mass, they may still be able to do it well. It just needs someone to cue them in, so they are not anxious about when to go up to read. Praise them afterwards. You could ask them to move chairs or wash coffee cups. Use your imagination.

Now is the time when it may be helpful for them to join in things they didn't before: a prayer group, a lunch club. Think about what your church can offer. Could you extend this invitation to those beyond your parish?

Over time, those with dementia will become less active. You may see them less often in church. Perhaps a group of you could get together and draw up a schedule for weekly visits. Don't just leave it to the clergy and pastoral visitors.

If they do not have transport, or have had to give up driving, take them out occasionally. As they become more disoriented, find out their favourite, familiar places and awaken happy memories by taking them there.

Don't let them be relegated to the list of the housebound you pray for but never visit.

As a church community, find out what you can do to make your church more dementia friendly.

God who has made the Church one Family,

you went out of your way to include those on the edges of society. May our doors and our hearts be open to all. Grant us the insight to see when one of our members is increasingly in need of help. Let us be quick to ask what we can do, and faithful in offering that support.

Give us the wisdom to see the person with dementia as you see them: as a unique individual, valued and loved. Let us not write them off because they have a disability. Show us the many ways in which they can still be part of our community, and the avenues of service still open to them. Guide us to show them new ways in which they can be valued.

It's easy to overlook them. May we make time in our busy lives to include them and assure them of our continued love.

Save us from leaving the care of those with dementia to the clergy and pastoral visitors. Teach us to be a dementia friendly church.

Acknowledgements

My grateful thanks to those who have read this book and made helpful suggestions, particularly Jack Priestley, Margaret Farrow and Paula Baker. I am indebted to the many people who have shared their experiences with me. My gratitude to the National Health Service, to the Alzheimer's Society and to all those, professionals, volunteers and friends, who have given generous help in my own situation.